CONTENTS

PREFACE

by Betty Comden & Adolph Green

A phone call from George Abbott always held promise of excitement. Late in 1952, I (Betty) got a phone call and it was George asking if we could write the lyrics for a show based on *My Sister Eileen* to star Rosalind Russell. I (Adolph) was in Paris and got a call from me (Betty) telling about it, which caused me (Adolph) to rush home at once. It seems they had a partial score they were unsure of. George asked if we could write a score in four weeks because after that they would lose Miss Russell to other commitments, and wanted to know what composer we could suggest. We thought of Leonard Bernstein, knowing he had just returned from his honeymoon with Felicia, and mentioned him dubiously to George. George said: "Go over and ask him right away!" We did, although we were very doubtful if Lenny would be interested. Among other things he had promised his mentor Serge Koussevitsky that after *On the Town* he would get down to serious business and never, never write another show. We had no sooner entered Lenny's apartment and were blurting out the facts about the show when the phone rang. It was George, never one to waste time, barking at us impatiently, "Well, is it yes or no?!!" To our surprise, with no hesitation Lenny said "Yes." He always liked deadlines, and four weeks to write a score was an irresistible challenge.

The play by Joseph Fields and Jerome Chodorov written in the 1940's had been based on stories by Ruth McKenney about two girls from Columbus, Ohio, who come to New York in the mid-30's to seek fame and fortune. We resisted all pressure to update it to the 50's, and knew we were on our way when Lenny exuberantly banged out on the piano the Eddie Duchin vamp, a characteristic musical sound of the 1930's. We were creatively on our way to Greenwich Village and adventure in the "Big City," and were able to complete the score in the prescribed four weeks.

This show celebrates New York as the magnet for young people from all fields of endeavour who, like Ruth and Eileen, still come here to fulfil their aspirations in this Wonderful Town.

from *The New York Musicals of Comden & Green*
© 1997 by Betty Comden & Adolph Green (Applause Theatre Books, New York).
Reprinted by permission

PLOT SYNOPSIS

ACT ONE

Wonderful Town is set largely in Greenwich Village, that agreeable maze that isn't what it used to be, and probably never was. The time is the summer of 1935, and a guide is showing tourists the sights on Christopher Street. Ruth and Eileen Sherwood appear, fresh off the train from Ohio, and are tricked into renting a dismal basement apartment. Between visits from the clientele of the former tenant (a lady of dim virtue) and the blasting beneath for a new subway, Ruth and Eileen spend a grisly night, and wish they had stayed behind in "Ohio." The next day, Eileen, a blonde knockout, finds herself surrounded by suitors almost immediately, as usual, while Ruth, a would-be writer, attractive but lacking in confidence, is ignored. Ruth explains her system for "One Hundred Easy Ways to Lose a Man."

Ruth takes her manuscripts to the offices of a magazine edited by Bob Baker. He bluntly tells her that her melodramatic pieces are bad, and that she should write about things she has experienced. He laments the waste of talent in New York ("What a Waste"). Later, feeling sorry for his gruffness with Ruth, he finds the apartment and meets Eileen, who at once falls "A Little Bit in Love" with him. Another visitor is the Wreck, a former atheclete who is not exactly married to the girl who shares his lodgings. He is still dazzled by his college fame in football ("Pass That Football"), but does excellent ironing, and being unemployed makes himself helpful around the place. Ruth shows up and invites Baker for dinner, to which Eileen has invited Frank Lippencott, a drugstore manager who showers her with gifts from the daily specials.

As dinner time approaches, Eileen appears with still another guest, Chick Clark, a brash young newspaper-man who is hotly pursuing her. The five make a game try at finding mutual interest but the evening breaks up in an argument and Baker muses that what he really wants is "A Quiet Girl."

Determined to be alone with Eileen, Chick invents a newspaper assignment for Ruth, who dashes off to the Brooklyn Navy Yard to interview a group of Brazilian cadets. They, however, have nothing on their minds but learning the conga, and follow the distraught Ruth back to her apartment, dancing all the way. Once they meet Eileen, they switch allegiance immediately and near-riot ensues as they conga their way through the Village.

ACT TWO

Eileen is arrested for disturbing the peace, but so charms the police at the precinct that they are virtually her slaves, even after learning that she is not Irish ("My Darlin' Eileen"). Ruth manages to get Eileen released, and doggedly takes a job walking through the streets with a sign advertising the Village Vortex, a nightclub, where the new sensation "Swing" can be heard. Eileen realizes Ruth loves Baker and convinces him that without knowing it he is in love with Ruth. Baker exuberantly expresses his feelings in "It's Love." It now appears that Ruth's story about the Brazilian Navy has won her a job, and Eileen in turn has been given a chance to sing at the Village Vortex, thanks to the notoriety her arrest has brought. Together with Ruth, she sings an old family favorite ("The Wrong Note Rag"). At the club Baker and Ruth find each other. For Ruth and Eileen, New York has indeed turned out to be a Wonderful Town.

© 1999 by Betty Comden and Adolph Green

WONDERFUL TOWN FACTS

ORIGINAL PRODUCTION

Opened February 26, 1953 at the Winter Garden Theatre, New York
559 performances
Produced by Robert Fryer. Directed by George Abbott. Choreography by Donald Saddler. Orchestrations by Don Walker. Musical Direction and Vocal Arrangements by Lehman Engel. Scenic and Costume Design by Raoul Pène Du Bois. Lighting Design by Peggy Clark.

Opening Night Cast:

Ruth	Rosalind Russell
Eileen	Edith Adams
Robert Baker	George Gaynes
Chick Clark	Dort Clark
Wreck	Jordan Bentley
Frank Lippencott	Cris Alexander

Awards
New York Drama Critics Award: Best Musical

Tony Awards: Best Musical; Best Actress (Rosalind Russell); Best Choreographer; Best Conductor and Musical Director; Best Scenic Designer

2003 REVIVAL

Opened November 23, 2003 at the Al Hirschfeld Theatre, New York
Produced by Roger Berlind and Barry and Fran Weissler. Directed by Kathleen Marshall.
Choreography by Kathleen Marshall. Orchestrations by Don Walker. Musical Direction and Vocal
Arrangements by Rob Fisher. Scenic Design by John Lee Beatty. Costume Design by Martin
Pakledinaz. Lighting Design by Peter Kaczorowski. Sound Design by Lew Mead.

Opening Night Cast:

Ruth Sherwood	Donna Murphy
Eileen Sherwood	Jennifer Westfeldt
Robert Baker	Gregg Edelman
Chick Clark	Michael McGrath
Wreck	Raymond Jaramillo McLeod
Frank Lippencott	Peter Benson

DISCOGRAPHY

Original 1953 Broadway Cast
Conductor: Lehman Engel
Principal Cast: Rosalind Russell, Edith Adams, George Gaynes
MCA 10050

1958 Television Cast
Conductor: Lehman Engel
Principal Cast: Rosalind Russell, Jacquelyn McKeever, Sydney Chaplin
Sony 48021

1986 London Cast
Conductor: David Steadman
Principal Cast: Maureen Lipman, Emily Morgan, Nicolas Colicos
Relativity 8260

1998 Studio Cast
Conductor: John Owen Edwards
Principal Cast: Karen Mason, Rebecca Luker, Ron Raines
Jay Records 1281

1999 Studio Cast
Conductor: Sir Simon Rattle
Principal Cast: Kim Criswell, Audra McDonald, Thomas Hampson
EMI Classics 56753

2003 Broadway Revival Cast
Conductor: Rob Fisher
Principal Cast: Donna Murphy, Jennifer Westfeldt, Gregg Edelman
DRG Records 12999

Ohio
(Duet)
Ruth and Eileen

Lyrics by
BETTY COMDEN
and **ADOLPH GREEN**

Music by
LEONARD BERNSTEIN

EILEEN:
Oh, Ruth!

RUTH:
Now, Eileen, everything's going to be all right.

EILEEN:
It's awful!

RUTH:
Never mind, Eileen,
try and sleep.

EILEEN:
I *can't* sleep.

RUTH:
Try, darling,
make your mind
a blank.

EILEEN:
I did, but I
keep thinking
of Ohio.

Slowly (flowing)

EILEEN: *(plaintively)*
Why,___ oh why,___ oh why, oh,___

RUTH:
8 lower, if possible - - - - - - - - - -
Why,___ oh why,___ oh why, oh,___

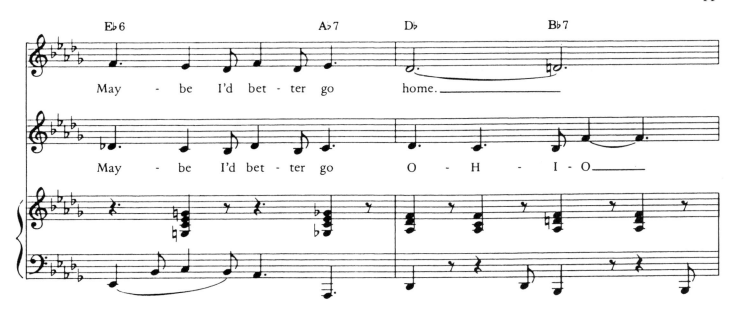

May - be I'd bet - ter go home.

May - be I'd bet - ter go O - H - I - O

May - be I'd bet - ter go home.

May - be I'd bet - ter go home.

RUTH:
Now

A la Shep Fields

lis - ten, Ei - leen,__ O - hi - o was stif - ling. We just could - n't wait_ to get

12

EILEEN:

out of the place,__ With Mom say-ing,"Ruth,__what no date for this eve — ning? And

BOTH: RUTH:

Pop with, "Ei - leen,__ do be home, dear, by ten."   Ugh!   The

EILEEN:

gos - sip - y neigh-bors And eve - ry - one yap - ping who's go - ing with who,__ And

RUTH: EILEEN:

dat - ing those drips__that I've known since I'm four.__ The Ki - wan - is Club Dance.__On the

14

One Hundred Easy Ways

Ruth

Lyrics by
**BETTY COMDEN
and ADOLPH GREEN**

Music by
LEONARD BERNSTEIN

*(Sing in a spirit of
rueful self-mockery)*

(Spoken flatly)
"Just get out, crawl under the car, tell him it's the gasket, and fix it in two seconds flat with a bobby pin."

bat your eyes and say, "What a ro-man-tic spot we're in."

That's a good way to lose a man. He takes you to the base-ball game, you

sit knee to knee, He says, "The next man up at bat will bunt you'll see." Don't

Just say, "Bunt? Are you nuts?! With one out, and two men on base, and a left-handed batter coming up, he'll walk right into a triple play, just like it happened in the fifth game of the World Se-ries in 1923."

say, "Oooh, what's a bunt? This game's too hard for lit-tle me."

18

That's a sure way to lose— a man,— A sure, sure, sure, sure

way to lose a man, A splen-did way—— to lose a man.— Just throw your

knowl-edge in his face, He'll nev-er try for sec-ond base.

Nine-ty-eight ways to go, The third way to lose— a man,—— The

19

20

What a Waste

Ruth, Baker, and Editors

Lyrics by
BETTY COMDEN
and ADOLPH GREEN

Music by
LEONARD BERNSTEIN

And their sto-ries all fol-low one line,

(pointing to First Editor) (pointing to Second Editor) (pointing to himself with both hands)

Like his, Like his, Like mine! __

Bouncy (♩ = 84)

1. (Baker) Born in Du-luth, __
2. (First Editor) Man from De-troit, __

Nat-u-ral writ-er, Pub-lished at sev-en— gen-i-us type. __
Won-der-ful art-ist, Went to Pi-cas-so— Pab-lo said, "Wow!" _

waste of mon - ey and time!

3. (Second Edtor) Girl from Mo - bile, __ Ver - sa - tile ac - tress,
4. (Baker) Kid from Cape Cod, __ Fish - er - man's fam - 'ly,

Trag - ic or com - ic, An - y old play. __ Suf - fered and starved, __
Mar - vel - ous sing - er– Big bar - i - tone. __ Rent - ed his boat, ___

Met Stan - i - slav - sky. He said the world __ would cheer her some - day. __
Paid for his les - sons, Starved for his stud - ies, Down to the bone. __

A Quiet Girl*

Baker and Men's Chorus

Lyrics by
BETTY COMDEN and ADOLPH GREEN

Music by
LEONARD BERNSTEIN

* Original key was a minor third lower.

A Little Bit in Love

Eileen

Lyrics by
BETTY COMDEN
and ADOLPH GREEN

Music by
LEONARD BERNSTEIN

haps a lit - tle bit more.

(rhythmically)

When he — looks at me — ev - 'ry-thing's ha - zy and all out of fo - cus.

When he — touch - es me — I'm in the spell of a strange ho - cus po - cus.

It's so — I don't know, — I'm so — I don't know, — I don't

40

Pass That Football
Wreck

Lyrics by
BETTY COMDEN
and ADOLPH GREEN

Music by
LEONARD BERNSTEIN

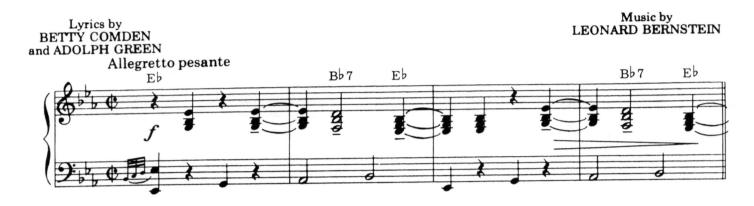

Allegretto pesante

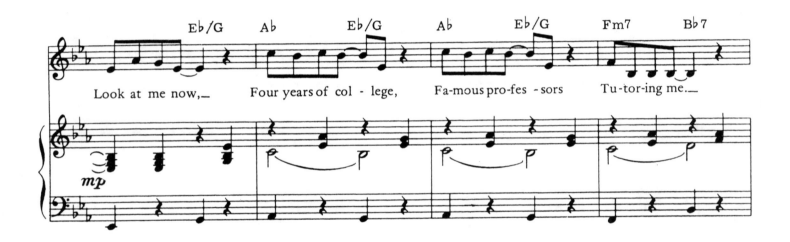

Look at me now,___ Four years of col - lege, Fa-mous pro-fes - sors Tu-tor-ing me.___

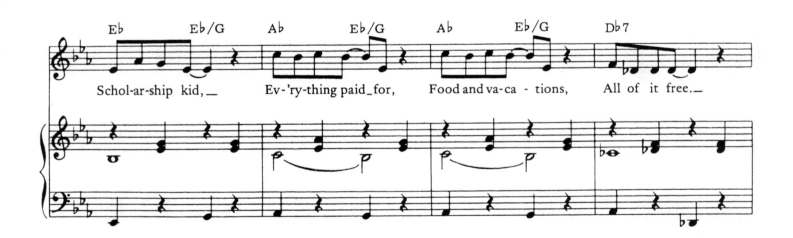

Schol-ar-ship kid, ___ Ev-'ry-thing paid_for, Food and va - ca - tions, All of it free.___

44

My Darlin' Eileen

(Based on an Irish Reel)

Policemen and Eileen

Lyrics by
BETTY COMDEN and ADOLPH GREEN

Music by
LEONARD BERNSTEIN

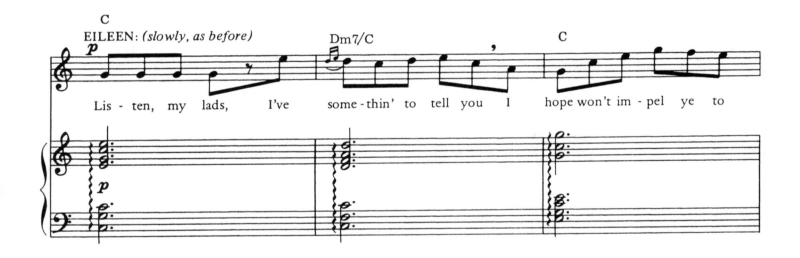

EILEEN: *(slowly, as before)*

Lis - ten, my lads, I've some-thin' to tell you I hope won't im - pel ye to

cry and to keen. Moth - er's a Swede, and Fa - ther's a Scot, And so

Dance
As before

Tutti, *shouting:*

Ei - leen!

Swing
Ruth and Villagers

Lyrics by
BETTY COMDEN
and ADOLPH GREEN

Music by
LEONARD BERNSTEIN

VILLAGER: Hey, cats, get a load of that square!

58

65

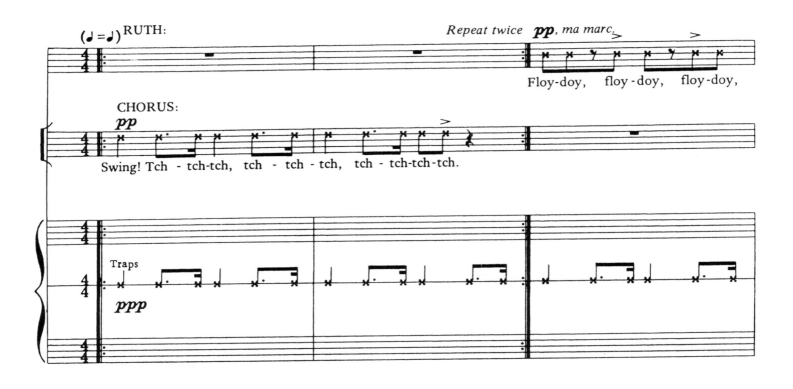

68

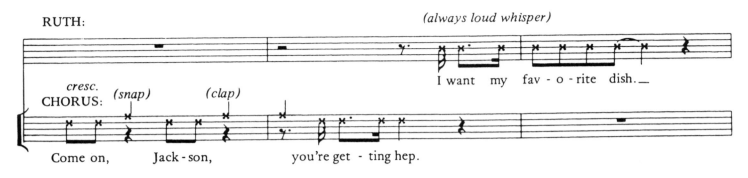

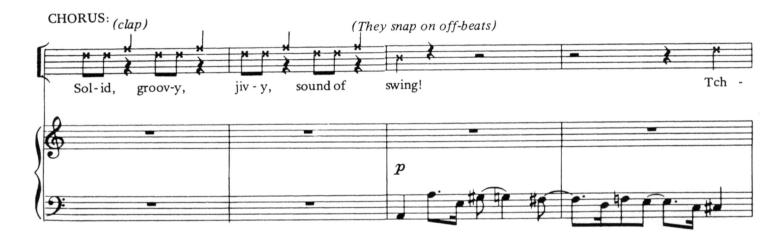

69

RUTH:

Down in the well,_ well, well, well My fa-vor-ite dish _ Ahh fish!

CHORUS:

[From offstage]

Ge -

(Her hands before her, mesmerized.)
[Exit.]

Thank you. Swing,_ swing,_ swing,_ swing,_

(sempre dim.)

sund-heit. You're wel-come. Swing,_ swing,_ swing,_ swing,_

sempre dim.

_ swing,_ swing!_

_ swing,_ swing!_

ff sub.

gliss. gliss.

sf

fff

long

sffz

It's Love

Eileen, Baker and Chorus

Lyrics by
BETTY COMDEN and ADOLPH GREEN

Music by
LEONARD BERNSTEIN

78

The Wrong Note Rag

Ruth, Eileen and Chorus

Lyrics by
BETTY COMDEN
and ADOLPH GREEN

Music by
LEONARD BERNSTEIN

* Ruth may sing one octave lower.

* These four bars may be shouted.